C000243952

SINEVVS OF WAR

**The Logistical Battle to Keep the 53rd Welsh Division
On the Move During Operation Overlord**

France – Holland – Belgium – Germany
June 1944 – May 1945

Major A. D. Bolland M.B.E.

Pen & Sword
MILITARY

This edition published in 2017 by

Pen & Sword Military
An imprint of
Pen & Sword Books Ltd.
47 Church Street
Barnsley
South Yorkshire
S70 2AS

This book was originally published as 'Team Spirit – The Administration of an Infantry Division during "Operation Overlord"' by Gale & Polden Ltd., Aldershot, 1948.

Copyright © Coda Publishing Ltd. 2017.
Published under licence by Pen & Sword Books Ltd.

ISBN: 9781473868564

A CIP catalogue record for this book is available from the British Library.

Printed and bound in England
By CPI Group (UK) Ltd., Croydon, CR0 4YY

Pen & Sword Books Ltd. incorporates the imprints of Pen & Sword Aviation, Pen & Sword Family History, Pen & Sword Maritime, Pen & Sword Military, Pen & Sword Discovery, Pen & Sword Politics, Pen & Sword Atlas, Pen & Sword Archaeology, Wharncliffe Local History, Wharncliffe True Crime, Wharncliffe Transport, Pen & Sword Select, Pen & Sword Military Classics, Leo Cooper, The Praetorian Press, Claymore Press, Remember When, Seaforth Publishing and Frontline Publishing

For a complete list of Pen & Sword titles please contact:

PEN & SWORD BOOKS LIMITED
47 Church Street, Barnsley, South Yorkshire, S70 2AS, England
E-mail: enquiries@pen-and-sword.co.uk
Website: www.pen-and-sword.co.uk

SINEWS OF WAR

CONTENTS

ILLUSTRATIONS

APPENDICES
MAPS AND GRAPHS

"The country, your companions, and the length of your journey will afford a hundred compensations for your toil." — OVID, *Remediorum Amoris*.

Normandy Road

"Where dust and
damn'd oblivion is
the tomb of honour'd
bones indeed."

SHAKESPEARE:
All's Well That Ends Well

PUBLISHERS' NOTE

*T*EAM SPIRIT – The story of the administration of the 53rd (Welsh) Division during Operation "Overlord" – was privately printed in Germany whilst the Division formed part of the British Army of the Rhine with the object of recording the detailed story of the Divisional Administration during its advance from the Normandy beachhead to the shores of the Baltic.

The original book had a limited edition which was circulated among members of the Division.

Such a story, full of facts and statistics of value to the historian and military student, is one which is of considerable interest and, although the story of one single division, it covers nearly every phase of military operations – a beachhead build-up following an assault landing – advance – opposed crossings – attack.

Here is a wealth of detailed information which gives some conception of the magnitude of administration of an army in the field. Here is "The School Solution" for the student on which to base his appreciation of administrative problems.

This edition contains certain modifications, and certain domestic details applicable only to the 53rd Division have been omitted. These omissions do not, however, detract from the main story. The facts are here in this up-to-date record of a division's administrative activities in a theatre of operations.

FOREWORD

This book tells the story of the administration of an Infantry Division of some 17,000 men which landed on the beaches of Normandy in June, 1944, and fought throughout the campaign in North-West Europe until reaching Hamburg in May, 1945. It tells, amongst other things, how these men were supplied with arms, ammunition, vehicles, food and petrol, how they were kept in action during those ten months, how many prisoners they took and how many of them became casualties. In brief, it tells you many of the facts which, although such an important part of a modern mechanised formation, are not normally recorded and published.

As the story of one Division only, it does not mention the achievements of those who were employed on the hundreds of miles of Lines of Communications, supplying the 21st Army Group as a whole, for these would make a far larger volume – it merely deals with those administrative services who, deployed within sound of the enemy's guns, bore on their battle-dress the same Divisional Sign as the men they were supplying. Perhaps the facts and figures which you will read in the following pages will give you some idea of the magnificent work done by these "men behind the lines" in their difficult and unspectacular task of providing the fighting troops with all that they required.

The book is humbly dedicated to the soldiers of the Royal Armoured Corps, the Royal Regiment of Artillery and the Infantry of the Line, for they were the backbone of the Divisional Team, and we will never forget it. Their battles cannot be covered in a few pages: they will be recorded for all time in Battle Honours and Regimental Histories. As Horace wrote in one of his odes – "Posterity shall hear of those battles."

In presenting this book to you I, as one who was privileged to serve for six years in a first-class team, and who is now searching for that same "team spirit" in civilian life, would like to offer my thanks to Captain B. St. C. Rutherford, who provided all the photographs, to Cpl. J. C.

Ogle, who drew all the sketches, and above all, to the officers, non-commissioned officers and men of the 53rd Welsh Division who made this story so well worth telling.

A.D.B.

August, 1946.

OPERATION OVERLORD
JUNE 1943 – MAY 1945

*F*rom Arromanches to Hamburg we travelled together in just over ten months of hard, almost non-stop, operations. The battles we fought during those ten months of Operation 'Overlord' will be recorded in history, and remain for us all a vivid memory of a period which we shall remember with pride for the rest of our lives.

Our object now is to present a few facts about the backroom activities of the Services of the 53rd Welsh Division, and as we pay tribute to their faithful work so also do we pay tribute to the Royal Army Medical Corps and the Royal Corps of Signals who, unheralded and unsung, have faithfully formed such an important part of the Divisional team.

On VE Day, Lieutenant-General Sir Neil Ritchie, Commander Xll Corps, with whom we were so closely associated throughout the campaign, wrote to the Divisional Commander and described the Division as 'a team in which every element has so fully played its part'. Victory in battle has proved the fine fighting qualities of our Infantry Battalions, the Reconnaissance Regiment, the Machine Gun Battalion, the Gunners and the Sappers. Let us now see how this victory was made possible by the Services and other arms who so ably and so cheerfully backed them up.

As the Divisional Commander, Major-General R. K. Ross, said in his Victory Order of the Day, 'Battles cannot be won without paying the cost and we have had heavy casualties.' The cost of this battle was indeed heavy, for we lost 9,849 Officers and Men killed, wounded and missing.

Further details of our casualties can be found in 'Paying the Cost'. Against this loss, however, we took a total of some 35,000 prisoners of war, not counting those 40,000 we rounded up in Hamburg and the number who passed through our medical installations; the German dead we have seen for ourselves on the battlefields of North-West Europe.

To achieve this success, the Royal Army Service Corps delivered to the guns some 1,318,800 rounds of 25-pdr. ammunition (roughly 21,000 tons or 7,000 3-ton lorry loads), and well over 400 tons of small arms ammunition.

To transport the Division into action, 4,343,037 gallons of petrol (17,700 tons) and 107,600 gallons of oil were used. Some 6,045,680 rations were issued which meant that as much as 14,363 tons of food were transported from the Corps Field Maintenance Centre to the Divisional Administrative area – an average distance of 45 miles. We can say, therefore, that during this campaign every man in the Division ate 17 cwt. of food – fourteen times his own weight! To keep everyone fighting fit, 352,000 rations of rum were issued – a total of 2,894 gallons, of which 1,228 gallons were consumed during Operation 'Veritable'. But astronomical figures are confusing to the layman, so we leave it to those who are interested to look at pages 45 to 49.

Those who have so often heard the clarion call of Ordnance 'Not Available', may be interested to learn that 409 motorcycles, 263 jeeps, 295 15-cwt. trucks, 255 3-ton lorries and 383 carriers were produced out of the Ordnance hat.

Other items brought over the hundred of miles of Lines of Communications were 276 2-in. mortars, 653 Bren guns, 254 Ps.I.A.T., 441 mine detectors – not to mention the more attractive items which had consistently good sales – 2,317 watches, G.S., 673 pairs of binoculars, 635 compasses, prismatic, and 1,030 portable cookers. As for spare parts, the total issue of scaled items made was 90.3 per cent of demands, a total of 120,455 issues of M.T., wireless, and armament spares.

On the clothing side, over 40,000 battle-dresses were issued, together with 113,693 pairs of socks, 34,200 caps, G.S., 29,000 shirts and 15,396 pairs of anklets, web. We could go on with this catalogue of Ordnance achievements, but feel that there is enough here to see that a situation which at the time seemed unpromising was *in toto* a fine effort. For fuller details see pages 52 to 55.

And what of the contribution made by the Royal Electrical and Mechanical Engineers to the advances? We shall always remember the alternate dust and slime of 'Ship', 'Bottle', and 'Hat' routes in the beach-head, the fantastic 'Moon' route through the Falaise pocket, the cobbled roads of Belgium (so harmful to the liver), the bogs of Holland, the ice and snow of the Ardennes, the mud and floods of the Reichswald Forest, and those appalling roads built by the ex-master race. Despite the severe shocks which all our vehicles have received throughout the campaign, R.E.M.E. never failed to keep us mobile, and their output has been out of all reasonable proportion to any civilian garage working under ideal conditions.

L.A.Ds. alone repaired 555 vehicles damaged by enemy action and 6,250 which had broken down through other causes, whilst the total number of vehicles repaired by the Divisional R.E.M.E. resources came to just under 11,000. It is clear then that, as civilians, we owe to R.E.M.E. a debt of gratitude to the extent of hundreds of thousands of pounds. And as for the guns which never failed to support our infantry despite the enormous number of rounds fired, 63 were repaired after damage from enemy action and 696 were repaired from other defects. If these figures are interesting, turn to page 60.

OPERATION "OVERLORD" ROUTE

The record of the Royal Corps of Signals throughout the campaign has spoken for itself (particularly on the air). Throughout the whole campaign the Divisional Command net was closed for a total of thirty days and worked without a break for 5,952 hours. The average number of telephone calls made per week of the operation was 6,773 (968 per day or 40 per hour for each 24 hours) – and this on the main Divisional switchboards alone.

The D.R.L.S. and its young cousin the S.D.S. travelled 475,114 miles – or nineteen times round the world, whilst the amount of cable laid by all companies of Divisional Signals would stretch from Lisbon to Singapore – a distance of 7,347 miles! On the equipment side, Signals issued 547 wireless sets, 162 charging sets, and 262 telephones: but to continue this catalogue turn to pages 69 to 72.

Throughout the campaign we have watched with pride the magnificent work done at all hours of the day and night by the Regimental Medical Officers and the Medical Officers and Staffs of Field Ambulances and Field Dressing Stations. How many owe their lives to their skill and attention no one can say, but the figures given in "Paying the Cost" give you some idea of the very great achievements of our Divisional R.A.M.C.

Briefly, the total number of battle casualties and sick and exhaustion cases who passed through our medical installations was 15,074, an average of 350 per week. Of this total, more than half (8,850) were sick and exhaustion cases.

Only on two days during the campaign were no casualties admitted (on 5th September, 1944, just before the Division entered Belgium, and on 19th January, 1945, the day on which we moved to the Eindhoven

area prior to Operation 'Veritable'). The four busiest days were on 11th February, 1945 (D+3 of Operation 'Veritable'), 1st March, 1945 (at Goch), 14th August, 1944 (at Bois Halbout just after the crossing of the Orne) and on 6th January, 1945 (in the Ardennes) when 290, 278, 255 and 253 casualties respectively were admitted to Field Ambulances or Field Dressing Stations. The number of officers and men reporting sick throughout the campaign was 7,313 – an average of 23, or .135 per cent of the Division, per day. It is not possible to give particulars of the work done by the Field Hygiene Section. The fitness figures bear testimony to their work.

The story of our movements during the campaign is told in 'The Road to Victory'. From the beaches of Normandy to Hamburg we travelled some 1,937 miles (or to draw another parallel, half the distance from Hamburg to New York). Our longest move was in September, 1944, when we travelled 108 miles from Gheluvelt to Antwerp: other notable moves took place on 19th January, 1945 (95 miles from Tilff in the Ardennes to Nuenen in Holland), and on 9th April when we moved 80 miles from Westerkapeln to Riethausen. We passed the 1,000-mile mark on 27th December, 1944, just after spending our forlorn Christmas at Mettet. No records have been kept of the total number of maps issued during the campaign, but it may be of interest to know that during Operation 'Veritable' alone 250,000 were supplied to units of this Division.

There are numerous other activities which have been going on behind the lines, all of which have their own story to tell, but which would make this brief account into a book of considerable size. The continual arrival of reinforcements, the numbers of soldiers going on leave, the shows given in all kinds of places and all kinds of weathers by the Divisional Concert Party, and so on – so many are there that we can only give you a brief idea of them in 'The Rest of the Team'. One particular branch of these many 'personnel' services of the Division is, however, worthy of mention here – the Field Cash Office. During Operation 'Overlord', Wightman's Bank issued a total of £1,806,158 – which may be broken down into 23,911,277 French francs, 92,848,103 Belgian francs, 4,582,536 Dutch guilders, and 14,519,124 German marks; but only the Field Cashier can deal with such astronomical figures.

We hope that in this résumé of what went on behind the lines of the 53rd Welsh Division there is sufficient evidence to show how true were those words written by General Ritchie. We were, indeed, a team in which every element so fully played its part.

THE ROAD TO VICTORY

*"The Sunday contemplation of my travels, which, by often
rumination, wraps me in a most humorous sadness."*
SHAKESPEARE: *As You Like It*

*L*et us turn now for a few moments to look back on those ten
months. Let us look back at that long road along which we
travelled – a road now dusty, now a quagmire, now narrow, now broad,
now rough, now smooth – a road of many names: 'Ship', 'Hat', 'Bottle',
'Spade', 'Club', 'Diamond', 'Sun', 'Moon', 'Comet' – all to become the
Second Army's main highway into the heart of Nazi Germany – '240
U.P.'

At the end of this section you will find a list of towns and villages of
four European countries. They are the locations occupied by Divisional
Headquarters, and they tell the story of a Division which, untried in
battle, landed on the beaches of Normandy on 27 June, 1944 (D+21)
and fought for over ten months until it came to its journey's end at
Hamburg on 4 May, 1945.

THE INITIATION

As we cast our memories back to those hot June days of 1944 and look
back along that road we see the initial concentration of the Division in a
densely packed area South-West of Bayeux. A concentration which had
scarcely been completed before the sudden switch to meet an emergency
in the south-east of the beach-head forced us into relentless battle at a
moment's notice.

And there, on those gently undulating slopes of Normandy, we see
quiet villages now no more than heaps of rubble, but once the scenes
of many of our toughest battles. Such names as Putot-en-Bessin, St.

Mauvieu, Le Bon Repos, Evrecy, Bougy, Grainville, Le Cahier and Point 112 are indeed written deep in the memories of all of us.

Turning away from that month of horror and sustained casualties we see the enemy's resistance to the bridge-head suddenly giving way. The 'Caen Hinge' has been broken and we see the pursuit of a reeling enemy across the Odon and the Orne, as slowly but methodically we advanced towards Falaise, through close, difficult country, strewn with many mines.

NORMANDY

"The village sleeps, a name unknown, till men
With life-blood stain its soil, and pay the due
That lifts it to eternal fame, – for then
'Tis grown a Gettysburg or Waterloo."

HOWE: *Destinction*

'Ship' Route – Evrecy

'But the Ship it carries
me long, long ways,
An' draws far places
near.'

J.J. BELL:
On the Quay

FALAISE

"Then more fierce
The conflict grew; the din of arms, the yell
Of savage rage, the shriek of agony,
The groan of death, commingled in one sound
Of undistinguished horrors."

SOUTHEY: *Madoc in Aztlan*

The world remembers Falaise, but only those of us who were there remember the scenes of devastation of a beaten enemy – the wreckage of vehicles, tanks, and horse-drawn guns, the stenching carnage of man and beast.

We recall the hectic chase of a disorganised enemy, the crossing of the River Seine at the end of August, the almost romantic drive across Northern France and Belgium, with its cheering crowds, welcoming banners and fruitful gifts with which the liberated people of Western Europe greeted us, and the end of the first phase of our campaign when, on 6th September, we entered Antwerp, where for a few brief days the Division shared, even at Action Stations, the joys of a newly liberated city.

AUTUMN

Our thoughts turn next to those grim days which followed the gallant allied Airborne landings at Eindhoven, Nijmegen and Arnhem: the days when our troops struggled to widen the corridor betweenthe Escaut and the Wilhelmina Canals. And if most of us automatically think of those Dutch villages amongst which Voorheide, Reusel, Netersel and Middlebeers are numbered, our Sappers surely recall more vividly the

Nijmegen Bridge

"Beneath me flows
the Rhine, and, like
the stream of Time, it
flows amid the ruins
of the past."

LONGFELLOW:
Hyperion

's-Hertogenbosch Battlefield

"Who asks whether the enemy were defeated by strategy or valour?"

VERGIL: *Æneid*

countless waterways they bridged. For years to come peaceful traffic will be crossing the numerous bridges they built: testimonies of fine bridge-building in the face of all the perils of war.

And so from that damp and miserable spell on the "Island" North of Nijmegen we turn towards what was to be the scene of one of the Division's finest triumphs – 's-Hertogenbosch: "A brilliant capture" the Army Commander called it.

From the front line troops to the R.A.S.C. drivers, from Company Headquarters at Nuland to Divisional Headquarters at Oss, from Battalion Headquarters to "H.Q. Adm. Group" and its windmill, all played their part. Long will the name of the 53rd Welsh Division be remembered in 's-Hertogenbosch, and the significance of the occasion is perpetuated in a shield presented by the Division to the people of 's-Hertogenbosch on the first anniversary of the battle.

Without respite we were switched to the British Army's eastern flank to counter an enemy threat across the Deurne Canal. November days produced November conditions, and there followed six weeks of hard slogging over a wet and unkind countryside: from the Wessem Canal to the River Maas, from Stramproij to Roermond.

WINTER

We remember how during those long December nights we drew back into Belgium around Herentals to prepare for a new and even mightier thrust against the enemy, and how suddenly our plans were changed by

Ardennes Scene

"Now is the winter of our discontent."

SHAKESPEARE:
Richard III

Reichswald Forest

"The ruthless, vast,
and gloomy woods."

SHAKESPEARE:
Henry VI (Part 3)

Von Rundstedt's offensive in the Ardennes. On a dark and foggy night we moved back to Tervueren and the line of the River Dyle covering Brussels, and there we prepared to spend our Christmas Day. But at a moment's notice we moved off in the early dawn of 25th December to meet the enemy: for many of us there were to be no Christmas Dinners this year, only cold "Bully" in a slit trench. We shall remember that in Christmases to come.

It was intensely cold as British and American troops, side by side in that mountainous, icebound country of the Ardennes south of the River Meuse between Liége and Namur, steadily drove the enemy back. Soon the enemy's offensive had been broken, and we pulled back to Liége – to spend a fortnight under an incessant rain of V1 bombs. And so to Holland once more, to concentrate near Eindhoven, Nuenen and Helmond, and to prepare for our offensive which had been so rudely interrupted.

THE BEGINNING OF THE END

And now we see once more that grey, damp morning of 8th February, 1945, when, under a barrage of 1,000 guns firing three-quarters of a million shells, we and the many other Divisions grouped under the First Canadian Army started the memorable Operation "Veritable." As we

waited at Groesbeek for zero hour we saw standing gaunt before us the vast Reichswald Forest, long regarded by the Germans as impregnable, separated from us by flat, sodden country with a network of ditches. If the fighting was hindered by the appalling conditions so too was our maintenance. There were no metalled roads and all movement of ammunition and supplies and the evacuation of wounded took place along tracks already wet and unreliable, rapidly becoming morasses of mud and water.

Alone of all the Divisions which had opened the offensive, it fell to the lot of the 53rd Welsh Division to fight on without a break to within sight of the Rhine. As we think of this grim month we think of another list of names which we shall never forget – Frasselt, Materborn, Goch, Weeze, Kevelaer, Geldern, Issum and Alpon.

THE LAST LAP

A brief spell in Brussels provided a welcome rest for all except the Gunners, Sappers and R.A.S.C. who were busy preparing for action before the crossing of the Rhine and the final stage of our campaign – the advance across Westphalia. Our memory takes us across the Rhine at

Xanten, through glider-strewn Hamminkeln, through Bocholt, through that corner of Holland at Winterswijk where we spent Good Friday, to Vreden,

Ochtrup and Ibbenburen. Across the Rivers Aller and Weser we again won battle honours: of the fighting around Rethem General Sir Miles Dempsey said: "You fought like tigers, and by winning the battle as you did you opened the way for the Second Army to get straight through to the Elbe and so to the Baltic. I have placed this last  battle of yours very high: it was a most decisive victory."

And finally our recollection takes us to the fighting near Rothenberg and the Hamburg – Bremen Autobahn, resulting in the capture of over 11,000 prisoners since the crossing of the Rhine one month earlier. This was the Division's last battle, but the planning for the assault on Hamburg went on, and as we planned we dumped vast quantities of ammunition and emergency reserves of rations, as we had dumped them countless times before. Happily the assault was never necessary, and it was on 4th May, 1945, that this Division, so proven in war, marched into Germany's second city, Hamburg.

Thus we come to the end of our recollections. We remember with sorrow our many comrades who fell by the side of the road over which we have travelled, and we remember with pride our achievements. Our Division, once Territorial but now fused with Regular and war-recruited units, had indeed stood the test.

Slow progress in the Reichswald

"Muddy, ill-seeming, thick, bereft of beauty."

SHAKESPEARE:
The Taming of the Shrew

Slow progress in the Ardennes

"O thou who chariotest to thy dark wintry bed."

SHELLEY:
Ode to the West Wind

LOCATIONS OCCUPIED BY THE DIVISION

Date			Place	Total Miles
June	17	FRANCE	Subles (Bayeux)	7
	23	—	St. Amator St. Andre	9
	30	—	Secqueville en Bessin	11
July	2	—	Putot-en-Bessin	13
	18	—	St. Mauvieu (Carpiquet)	17.5
Aug.	5	—	Mondrainville	21.5
	9	—	Maisoncelles sur Ajon	30
	12	—	St. Laurent de Condrel	38
	15	—	Bois Halbout	44
	16	—	St. Germain Langot	49.5
	18	—	Leffard Falaise	52.5
	21	—	Brieux	69
	26	—	Orville	91
	27	—	Le Bois Normand pres Lyre	114
	29	—	La Chappelle du Bois de Faulx	152.5
	30	—	Le Thuit	185.5
	30	—	St. Jean de Frenelle	195.5
	31	—	Gournay	216.5
Sept.	2	—	Donneville	285.5
	4	—	Le Souich	303
	4	—	Bethonsart	321
	5	—	Bully (Mazingarbe)	335
	6	—	Fleurbaix	357
	7	BELGIUM	Gheluvelt	379
	9		Antwerp	487
	16		Veerie	520
	17		Baelen	536.5
Oct.	20	HOLLAND	Bergeyk	558.5
	24		Eersel	568.5

Date			Place	Total Miles
	6		Grave	611.5
	9		Slijk Ewijk Oosterhout	626.5
Oct.	17	HOLLAND	Schaijk	649.5
	18	—	Nistelrode	657.5
	21	—	Oss	662.5
	24	—	Nuland	669.5
	27	—	Moelenhoek	674.5
	28	—	Nuland	679.5
	31	BELGIUM	Bocholt	747.5
Nov.	13	HOLLAND	Stramproij	762.5
	16	—	Swartbroek	770.5
	25	—	Heijthuizen	779.5
Dec.	17	BELGIUM	Herenthals	840.5
	21	—	Tervuren	890.5
	25	—	Mettet	945.5
	27	—	Tervuren	1,000.5
	30	—	Leignon	1,058.5
Jan.	2	—	Nettine	1,067.5
	3	—	Baillonville	1,072.5
	8	—	Tilff	1,182.5
	19	HOLLAND	Nuenen	1,213.5
Feb.	6	—	Mook	1,253.5
	11	—	Groesbeek (Reichswald Forest)	1,285.5
	16	GERMANY	Frasselt	1,267.5
	18	—	Palandswald	1,276.5
	24	—	Goch	1,283
Mar.	3	—	Kevelear	1,293
	5	—	Geldern	1,300
	12	BELGIUM	Aasche	1,430
	23	GERMANY	Kevelear	1,580
	26	—	Wardt	1,600

Date			Place	Total Miles
	27	—	Kopenhof	1,604
	28	—	Dingden	1,608
	30	—	Bocholt	1,615
	31	HOLLAND	Winterswyk	1,631
Apr.	1	GERMANY	Vreden	1,637
	2	—	Alstatte	1,645
	3	—	Ochtrup	1,660
	5	—	Elte	1,678
	7	—	Westerkapeln	1,700
	9	—	Riethausen	1,780
	10	—	Eystrup	1,789
	15	—	Westen	1,800
	16	—	Wittlohe	1,803
	21	—	Kleinzuheins	1,813
	22	—	Wittorf	1,828
	23	—	Bothel	1,835
	24	—	Scheessel	1,849
	29	—	Toppenstedt	1,899
	3	—	Worth	1,914
	3	—	Bergedorf	1,925
	4	—	Hamburg	1,937

… and as in years to come you look at this list of towns and villages, these words of Robert Burns will surely ring true:

"Still o'er these scenes my mem'ry wakes
And fondly broods with miser care;
Time but th' impression stronger makes
As streams their channels deeper wear."

SEE HOW THEY RAN!

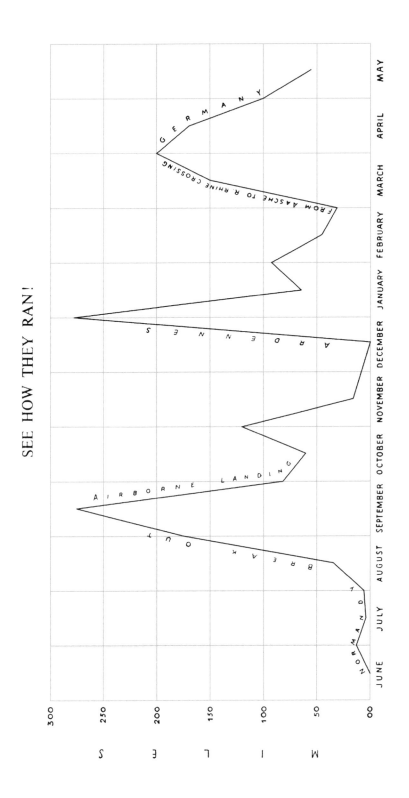

**Glider-strewn
Hamminkeln**

"How sweetly did
they float upon the
wings of silence
through the empty-
vaulted night."

Milton: *Comus*

Roermond Church,
Enemy O.P.

43

ROLL ALONG COVERED WAGON

"Victuals and Ammunition Are the Sinews of War."
JOHN HATCHER

This chapter tells, statistically and graphically, how the Royal Army Service Corps lived up to its name and enhanced its reputation by keeping hungry men, guns and vehicles supplied with all their needs throughout the campaign.

In normal circumstances an Infantry Division has four R.A.S.C. Companies and an R.A.S.C. Workshop to keep the vehicles on the road. The load-carrying vehicles are all 3-ton lorries, and the familiar red and green diagonal markings on them can be seen throughout the Army area, from artillery gun positions to the rear supply areas. Of the four Companies one is responsible for supplying food, one petrol and oil, and the other two carry 25-pdr. and small arms ammunition. Under arrangements made each day by the Divisional "Q" Staff in conjunction with H.Q.R.A.S.C., these Companies form supply, petrol and ammunition points to which Unit vehicles go to draw their daily requirements of these commodities. Gun ammunition is usually taken right on to the gun positions by the R.A.S.C. vehicles themselves.

As everyone knows, the rapid advances through France and Belgium stretched the administrative capacity of 21st Army Group to the utmost, and it was during this period that the R.A.S.C. did really magnificent work. Although this book does not attempt to extol the efforts of the Army as a whole, we must mention all those R.A.S.C. drivers who achieved the well-nigh impossible task of bringing forward all our requirements from the base in Normandy to the fighting zone in Belgium and Holland.

Our Divisional R.A.S.C. was not designed for long journeys to the rear areas, but nevertheless it often became necessary for it to go back to the Army Road Head to bring supplies forward to the Corps Field Maintenance Centre, which in its turn was usually about twenty-five miles behind the Divisional area – sometimes farther.

At times transport was so stretched that it was necessary for unit transport to be pooled for the collection of these vital supplies, and in this section we must not forget the excellent work done by quartermasters and all lorry drivers in this respect.

All in all, it speaks very highly for all concerned with supplies, petrol and ammunition that not on one single occasion throughout the campaign did the fighting troops go short of what they needed. There were indeed some nerve-wracking moments, but all was always well in the end. For this we must all thank the Royal Army Service Corps for tireless efficiency in their never-ending responsibilities of keeping us, our vehicles and our guns well fed.

TOTAL AMMUNITION ISSUES

SMALL ARMS		MORTARS	
Mk. VIIIZ	6,179,400	3-in. mortar H.E.	176,854
.303 Ctn.	3,786,656	4.2-in. mortar H.E.	96,250
.303 Bdr.	3,582,992	2-in. mortar H.E.	52,494
9-mm. Sten	2,935,700	2-in. mortar SMK	37,278
.303 Tracer	712,620	3-in. mortar SMK	18,596
.303 Incendiary	289,536	3-in. mortar Ill.	18,216
P.I.A.T. H.E.	20,340	2-in. mortar Ill.	18,126
		4.2-in. mortar SMK	3,416

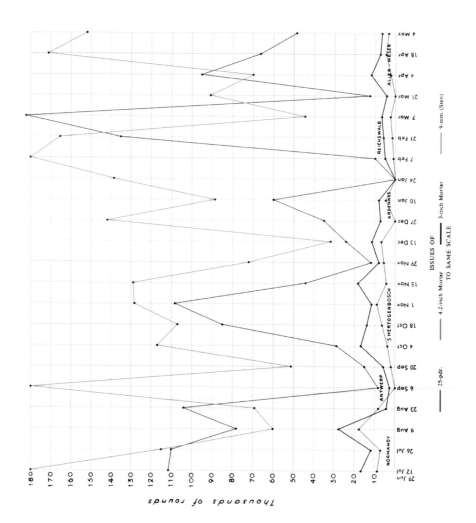

GUNS		MINES AND GRENADES	
25-pdr. H.E.	1,318,793	36 grenades	45,012
25-pdr. SMK	94,629	75 grenades	36,492
25-pdr. super carts	59,743	77 grenades	26,778
40 mm	49,168	Mines, A./Tank, Mk. V	11,455
6 pdr. A.P.C.B.C.	10,088		
6 pdr. S.A.B.O.T.	3,906		
17 pdr. A.P.C.B.C.	3,154		

NOTE: Total expenditure of 25-pdr. ammunition by 21 Army Group during Operation "Overlord" was 12,082,005 rounds.

"Give them great meals of iron and steel, they will fight like devils."
SHAKESPEARE, *Henry V.*

FOOD AND FUEL FACTS

SUPPLIES

Field Service Rations ....4,325,276 issued
Compo Rations..1,720,404 issued
Total Rations   6,045,680 issued
14,363 tons lifted
Rum..352,420 Rations (2,894 gallons) issued

PETROL, OIL AND LUBRICANTS

M.T. 80... 4,343,037 gallons
Oil .... 107,599 gallons
White Spirit .... 92,843 gallons
Derv. .... 77,775 gallons
Ethyleneglycol (anti-freeze) .... 7,686 gallons
Grease ....20,033 pounds

... and this is a sample of one month's turnover —

OPERATION "VERITABLE"

DETAILS OF PETROL ISSUED DURING PERIOD
8th FEBRUARY – 8th MARCH, 1945.

Date		Amount	Date		Amount
Feb.	8	15,439		22	13,774.5
	9	16,695		23	11,245.5
	10	8,334		24	14,287.5
	11	9,153		25	10,471.5
	12	14,210.5		26	10,471.5
	13	10,872		27	13,066.5
	14	11,826		28	13,396.5
	15	11,673	Mar.	1	9,886.5
	16	14,503.5		2	13,022
	17	12,091.5		3	10,661.5
	18	11,326.5		4	10,188
	19	7,281		5	9,693
	20	15,088.5		6	20,533.5
	21	15,156		7	13,945.5
					Total 348,293

"... Spirits are not finely touch'd – But to fine issues."
SHAKESPEARE: *Measure for Measure.*

DETAILS OF SUPPLIES ISSUED DURING PERIOD
8th FEBRUARY – 8th MARCH, 1945.

Item	Quantity	Rations
Field Service Rations	—	233,154
Compo.	25,150 packs	352,100
Rum	1,228 gallons	85,960
2-Man A.F.V.	1,321	2,642
3-Man A.F.V.	968 packs	2,904
Biscuits A.F.V.	5,546 tins	5,546
S./Heating Bev.	11,618 tins	11,618
24-hour packs	6,377 packs	6,377
Hexamine	35,160 tablets	—
Tommy Cookers	75	—
P.O.W. Rations	—	974

Total weight of Supplies lifted from F.M.Cs.:–
1,289 tons (approx.)

"An army, like a serpent, travels on its belly."
FREDERICK THE GREAT.

Second-Line Transport

1098 AND ALL THAT

"Put in their hands thy brusing irons of wrath."
SHAKESPEARE: *Richard III.*

As you turn over the next page or two you will see details of an astounding collection of articles of every imaginable description which were issued by the Royal Army Ordnance Corps during the campaign. A turnover of this nature would be the subject of considerable praise in any civilian establishment – if one could be found to deal with such a variety of items; but stop for a moment to think of the organisation required to bring all this equipment, much of it bulky, heavy, delicate, over such vast distances, so that it was always available when required, if essential for the winning of a battle or the morale of the troops. Articles less essential were naturally treated on a lower priority, and many of us grew accustomed to indents being returned "Not Available", but the figures overleaf show you just how essential demands were always met in full and how even less essential articles were very nearly in keeping with the demand.

Army Form G1098, as most who read this will know, is (in civilian language) the list of ordnance equipment to which a Unit is entitled and requires for operational needs. It follows that each type of Unit has its own requirements and the R.A.O.C. had to be conversant with every one of them. To keep every Unit supplied with its full G1098 was indeed a praiseworthy task. The photograph on page 56, taken during an advance in the early days in Normandy, gives you some idea of just how much G1098 equipment can be (and has to be) carried by that individual without whom no battle can be won – the Infantry soldier.

Before we leave the subject of Ordnance, we must not forget that tireless collection of men who were so often forgotten, so often despised, but such an essential part of the Army's morale – the Mobile Bath and Laundry Unit. You will see from the statistics that the laundry washed over 900,000 items of clothing whilst the bath unit bathed over 300,000 men. They certainly did more than their share in keeping the party clean!

ORDNANCE STATISTICS

VEHICLES

	Demanded	Issued
Motor cycles	419	409
Carriers and armoured O.Ps.	392	383
Trucks, 15-cwt.	310	295
Jeeps	270	263
Lorries, 3-ton	310	255
Tractors	86	86
Trailers	81	77
Cars, light recce.	57	57
Cars, heavy armoured	46	46
Cars, 2-seater	51	37
Ambulances	14	14
Cars, 4-seater	23	13
Cars, Scout	12	12

MAIN CLOTHING ISSUES

	Issued		Issued
Socks (pairs)	113,693	Caps, G.S.	34,202
Battle-dress trousers	46,628	Shirts	29,050
Battle-dress blouses	40,457	Anklets, web (pairs)	15,396
Boots, ankle	40,569	Greatcoats	5,304

GUNS, MORTARS AND SMALL ARMS

	Demanded	Issued
Bren guns	653	653
2-inch mortars	276	276
Ps.I.A.T.	254	254
Pistols	229	229
6-pdr. guns	40	40
Telescopic rifles	39	39
3-inch mortars	36	36
25-pdr. guns	35	35
Dischargers smk. gen.	31	31
Vickers M.Gs.	29	29
40 mm barrels	16	16
Besa M.Gs.	11	11
17-pdr. guns	11	11
4.2-inch mortars	10	10
25-pdr. barrels	8	8
40 mm S.P. guns	4	4
6-pdr. barrels	2	2

ISSUE OF M.T., SIGNAL AND WIRELESS AND ARMAMENT SPARES BY ORDNANCE FIELD PARK

Demands made 159,198

Issues made 120,455

Items not it stock... 12,806

Items not on sale 25,868

Percentage of issue of scaled items 90.3%

INSTRUMENTS, ETC.

	Demanded	Issued
Watches, G.S.	2,372	2,317
Binoculars	673	673
Compasses, prismatic	635	635
Mine detectors	441	441
Celluloid sheets	450	363
Watches, stop	17	17
Directors 7 B	11	7
Lighting Sets	6	6
Generator Sets	5	5
Rangefinders	6	5

SPECIAL WINTER ISSUES

Leather jerkins	17,900	Smocks, windproof	992
Oilskin oversuits	7,000	Boots, rubber thigh	807
Bivouacs (two men)	7,000	Stoves, oil, heating	800
Boots, rubber knee	6,833	Coats, Tropal	360
Coats, fur-lined	1,500	Coats, Jeep drivers'	340

NOTE: In addition 40 tons of snow camouflage equipment was held at Ordnance Dump for three months for immediate issue.

PORTABLE COOKERS ISSUED

No. 1...   ...113   No. 2...   ...668   No. 3...   ...249

LAUNDRY STATISTICS
Items Laundered

Towels	164,990	Vests	80,297
Socks (pairs)	156,101	Denim trousers	18,609
Shirts	149,844	Denim blouses	14,644
Drawers	147,733	Blankets	18,470

"Always washing, and never getting finished."
Hardy: *Tess of the D'Urbervilles.*

In addition, 307 Mobile Laundry and Bath Unit bathed 309,421 men (over 1,000 per day of the campaign).

"Do you think that I, then, am taking pleasure in my bath?"
Prescott: *Conquest of Mexico.*

G1098

"Battle's magnificently
stern array!"

BYRON:
Childe Harold

KEEPING THE WHEELS TURNING

"There are geniuses in trade, as well as in war."
EMERSON: *Essays.*

We come now to the Royal Electrical and Mechanical Engineers, offspring of the Royal Army Ordnance Corps and one of the Army's youngest children, having first seen the light of day during the early years of the recent war.

The Divisional R.E.M.E. resources consisted of three Brigade Workshops, one Light Anti-Aircraft Regimental Workshop and eleven Light Aid Detachments attached to Gunner Regiments, the Reconnaissance Regiment, Infantry Brigade Headquarters, Sappers and Signals. The Workshops, as their name implies, carried out the major repair and assembly operations, whereas the L.A.Ds. were responsible for running repairs and keeping vehicles, guns and equipment of all natures in good order.

To the layman it was a wonderful sight to see the manner in which whole garages would suddenly pack up and move off at a moment's notice, taking with them all the various vehicles and guns which were under repair, and as soon as they arrived at their new location – probably just another field – would set up shop again just as if nothing had happened.

In assessing the work of R.E.M.E., one must remember that, apart from anything else, every vehicle or gun which they kept on the road, or put back in action after being severely damaged by enemy action,

GIVE —
"Have we done this?"
SHELLEY: *The Cenci*

— AND TAKE

"An enemy hath done this."

St. Matthew

saved the tax-payer hundreds, if not thousands, of pounds. A total of over 10,000 vehicles repaired, when viewed in this light, is indeed an excellent performance.

To all ranks of the Royal Electrical and Mechanical Engineers, and especially to their private soldiers, known as craftsmen, the Army owes yet another debt of gratitude which cannot be expressed adequately. But for the speed and efficiency with which they repaired our vehicles and equipment many successful battles might well have turned against us and the war might have been prolonged considerably.

REME: GUN AND VEHICLE REPAIRS

	IN L.A.Ds.		IN WKSPS.		TOTAL		
	Enemy Action	Other Causes	Enemy Action	Other Causes	Enemy Action	Other Causes	Grand Total
Guns	19	300	44	396	63	696	759
Vehicles	555	6,250	238	3,858	793	10,901	10,901

ISSUES MADE BY WORKSHOPS
STORES SECTIONS

Miscellaneous 37,000
Engines...1,555
Gearboxes 496
Radiators 395
Rear axles...102
Transfer boxes 72
Front axles 53

Total issues 39,673

"Copper for the craftsmen cunning at his trade."
RUDYARD KIPLING: *Cold Iron.*

"A Tradesman thou! and hope to go to Heav'n?"
Persius: *Satires*

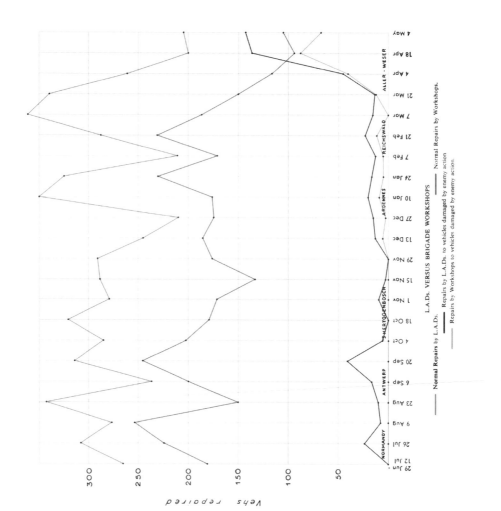

L.A.Ds. VERSUS BRIGADE WORKSHOPS

————— Normal Repairs by L.A.Ds.   ————— Normal Repairs by Workshops.

————— Repairs by L.A.Ds. to vehicles damaged by enemy action

————— Repairs by Workshops to vehicles damaged by enemy action.

Vehs repaired

THE REST OF THE TEAM

*"'Tis the sublime of man, our noontide majesty, to know
ourselves parts and proportions of one wondrous whole!"*
SAMUEL TAYLOR COLERIDGE: *Religious Musings.*

ONE MONTH IN THE LIFE OF THE SAPPER OPERATION "VERITABLE"

SUMMARY OF MAJOR R.E. WORK DURING PERIOD 8th FEBRUARY – 8th MARCH, 1945

1. BRIDGING

   12 Bridges constructed – 111 x 3 ton loads (800 ft. run bridge or 350 tons of bridging equipment).

   *"It is strange men cannot praise the bridge they go over,
   or be thankful for favours they have had."*
   ROGER NORTH: *Examen.*

2. ROAD REPAIRS

   3,200 tons brick rubble loaded and placed by hand 1,000x3 ton loads.
   200 yards Corduroy road   40x3 ton loads.
                                                                     <u>1,040</u>

3. MINE CLEARANCE

   54 miles of road and verges checked for mines – Countless mines lifted.

4. BULLDOZERS

   5 Bulldozers averaged 6 hours per day for 26 days – 780 Bulldozer hours. 20 major eraters filled.

Folding Boat Bridge (Escaut Canal)

"Don't cross the bridge till you come to it, Is a proverb old, and of excellent wit."

– LONGFELLOW: *The Golden Legend*

High Level Bailey Bridge (Dusseldorf)

"The Rhine, the Rhine, the German Rhine! Who guards today my stream divine?."

SCHNECKENBURGER: *Die Wacht am Rhein*

5. WATERPOINTS

9 Waterpoints established.

450,000 gallons water filtered, chlorinated and delivered.

"When they are thirsty, fools would fain have drink."
SHAKESPEARE: *Love's Labour Lost.*

11 FIELD SECURITY SECTION

"Our Watchworld is Security."
WILLIAM PITT.

Never designed or equipped to operate as a self-contained unit, without drivers or an Army Cook, the small section of 1 Officer and 12 N.C.Os. nevertheless worked from Normandy to Hamburg independently of any other headquarters or Unit.

In the course of the section's activities, which were designed to protect the entire Division from spies, saboteurs and subversive influences, the following figures are worthy of note:

158 Security Targets searched, two of which had to be de-booby-trapped, hundreds of documents sorted and removed.

21 safes opened with high explosive.

200 "collaborators" handed over to respective national authorities.

419 detailed interrogations carried out in French, Dutch, Flemish, German, Spanish, Russian, Danish and Norwegian.

374 persons arrested and sent to internment.

2 sabotage dumps discovered.

7 spies complete with radio transmitting sets and

3 saboteurs extracted from the thousands of refugees who were cursorily examined.

The registration of some 30,000 civilians organised and supervised.

THE DIVISIONAL PROVOST COMPANY

"Policeman are soldiers who act alone; soldiers
are policemen who act in unison."
HERBERT SPENCER: *Social Statics.*

The vanguard of the Division to land in Normandy shortly after D Day included a small band of Military Police headed by the A.P.M. Theirs was the task of paving the way for an easy landing and concentration of 17,000 men with their vehicles and stores in an area so congested that there was hardly room to swing even the proverbial cat! Thanks to perfect traffic control and first-class signing of routes by this small band of men the Division landed easily and in a remarkably short time was settled in its appointed concentration area with very few "strays" to be rounded tip.

In the early days of the campaign, the Provost Company with its 3 Officers and 109 Other Ranks, like the rest of the Division, began to feel its feet, suffer casualties, and generally settle down to the business of war for which it had so patiently trained and waited for five long years. Its tasks were varied: always there was traffic and movement which required close supervision – and who will forget that solitary pointsman who used to stand on the dusty cross-roads of shattered Cheux? – but in addition there were prisoners of war to be counted, searched and guarded in cages of capacity varying from 10 to 1,200; there were refugees to be escorted and directed to their nearest Civil Affairs Post; Security Duties at headquarters; anti-looting patrols; fifth-columnist scares to be investigated.

After the German débâcle in the Falaise Pocket, and the subsequent breakout to the Seine, life for the Military Policeman became a kaleidoscope of movement – "Sector Controls" leap-frogging ahead of each other, many times going ahead with nothing between themselves and the enemy – (a fact which did not come to light until later!) – keeping the Division's axis sign-posted so that it was almost an impossibility for anyone to lose his way. The familiar Divisional signs can still be seen along scores of roads in France and Belgium – souvenirs of the Road to Victory.

And so to Antwerp, with its patrolling to ensure that the "liberation" was not carried out too literally, to Lommel, Eindhoven, Nijmegen, 's Hertogenbosch, Weert, the Wessem Canal, the Ardennes, the Reichswald, the Rhine crossing, and the pursuit across the Westphalian plains and on to Hamburg. Summarised as they are, these movements seem small, but each one, be it river crossing, slow advance on ice-bound or impassable roads, forest penetration, or rapid advance in open country, each was a distinct Operation for the Provost Company, each with its individual and peculiar "headache" or "snag", which, however serious, had to be overcome if the victories gained by our fighting troops were to be exploited to the full.

Although this book is not intended to cover the period following VE Day, it may perhaps interest you to have some idea of the tasks which face the Military Policeman in an occupied country. In Hamburg, for instance, "Riot Squads" and "Vice Squads" were organised to supplement the German Police, their main tasks being to stop looting by civilians of wine and food stores: occasionally there were gangs of youths to be rounded up or war criminals to be unearthed – all this was, of course, in addition to the normal requirements of the Military Police to patrol the city by day and night, to set up information posts, to sign routes through and in the city, and so on.

In peace as well as in war soldiers lose their way when visiting large towns, and often have to be redirected, sheltered and fed: the Military Policeman is their saviour – and it is he, too, who officiates at accidents, often supervises the disposal of casualties: he is expected to give and does give, information about everything and anything: he helps in the eternal struggle to maintain law and order: he is at everyone's beck and call day and night.

To our Provost Company we say "Well done, the Coppers."

ARMY POSTAL SERVICE

TRAFFIC HANDLED BY POSTAL UNIT FROM LANDING IN NORMANDY TO 31st AUGUST, 1945

INWARD MAIL		
Letters	4,553,000	3,190 Bags
Parcels	560,275	46,725 Bags
Registered items	113,500	—
Newspapers	823,600	2,942 Bags

OUTWARD MAIL		
Letters	4,195,300	2,800 Bags
Parcels	81,940	6,825 Bags
Registered items	45,195	—

"Let me hear from thee by letters."
SHAKESPEARE: *Two Gentlemen of Verona.*

SIGNAL SUCCESSES

"Evil communication corrupt good manners."
NEW TESTAMENT: *Corinthians.*

The importance of communications in modern warfare has long been stressed in military textbooks, but few who have not experienced the work of the Royal Corps of Signals in battle can appreciate the real scope and complexity of their work. To many, the telephone and the wireless set are taken for granted – they always work, and the person required is always at the other end – but how many stop to think just who makes good communications possible and how they become possible?

Although wireless has come to be considered as the "modern" method of communication, for it is a quick and easy method, it suffers from interference, range restrictions and lack of security: for these reasons the telephone still holds its own, and is of vital importance at all times. So it is that line parties are always to be seen in the forefront of the battle, laying lines from higher to lower formations and from brigades to units – theirs indeed is a thankless, never-ending task, particularly in days of rapid advances.

Operation "Overlord" provided Divisional Signals with every imaginable type of problem. Initially there was the task of ensuring first-class communications during the vital "build-up" stage in the beach-head: there was the "static" period near Caen, when our troops were fighting so doggedly in Cheux, Evrecy, Le Bon Repos, Bougy, Gavrus and so many other villages.

In these trying days line communications were used to the full and the maintenance problems which faced cable repair parties can only be described in fitting language by the signal-men themselves! Continually were lines being cut by enemy shell-fire, vehicles, cattle and the many other accoutrements of the battlefield. But the lines were always "through".

After the "break-out", as the momentum of the Division's advance increased, it became more and more necessary to rely on wireless – high-powered, complicated sets working from Divisional Headquarters to Corps Headquarters and Brigade Headquarters, and from Brigade Headquarters to Units – so complicated did our wireless "nets" become that to the layman they were quite incomprehensible! To wireless operators in C.Vs. (3-ton Command Vehicles), "Gin Palaces" or "trucks 15 cwt. ffw" (fitted for wireless) we owe a debt of gratitude for faultless communications throughout these difficult days and nights of ceaseless movement.

And so it went on throughout the campaign – wireless and line, line and wireless – sometimes working under the most adverse conditions imaginable: to such conditions the Ardennes, the Reichswald Forest, and the Seine, Rhine, Weser and Aller River Crossings bear ample testimony.

In this brief résumé of the work of Royal Signals, we can but touch lightly on the work of this great Corps. So far we have mentioned only the work of wireless operators and linesmen. Equally arduous and vital, but somewhat less glamorous, was the work of the exchange operators, ever polite and patient when dealing with sometimes impolite and impatient "subscribers", handling an average number of 6,773 calls per week on the Divisional Headquarters exchanges alone. And we remember, too, that hard-working band of men enciphering and deciphering countless secret cipher groups, we remember the message operators receiving messages by day and night, we remember the technicians of "M" Section repairing instruments so rapidly and efficiently, and almost above all, we remember the "D.Rs."

The Despatch Riders of Royal Signals had one of the most thankless tasks of all – theirs was the duty of delivering messages and orders to formations and units all over the Corps front. Whatever the weather, whatever the time of day or night, whether hungry or cold or wet, D.Rs. were always there, waiting cheerfully to deliver the vital Operation Orders, Administrative Orders, or Fire Plans. Always taken for granted, always unsung, theirs was indeed a first-class job.

The figures which follow may give you some idea of the work covered by Royal Signals during this campaign. But in so far as communications in general are concerned, they are perhaps misleading, for we must not forget that in addition to the Royal Corps of Signals, all units, whether they be Gunners, Sappers, Infantry, R.A.S.C. or R.E.M.E., had their own system of communications: most had their own wireless operators, linesmen, message operators, exchange operators and despatch riders, and to all these is due as much praise as we have accorded to our friends of Royal Signals: their achievements are not recorded in the following list.

SOME SIGNAL FACTS

Miles travelled by D.R.L.S. S.D.S.	474,114
Cipher groups deciphered	261,000
Cipher groups enciphered	161,000
D.R.L.S./S.D.S. packages registered	106,588
Code signs and Slidex worked in HQ. Signals office	76,360
Batteries charged by "M" Section	22,775
Miles of cable expended	7,347
Average no. of telephone calls on Division exchange per week	6,773
Average no. of Messages in H.Q. Signals office per week	6,008
Hours worked by Division Command net	5,952
Repairs by "Z" lorry (R.E.M.E. Telecommunications Section)	4,830
Hours worked by Division "Q" net	4,728
First line wireless repairs by "M" Section	2,784
Wireless sets issued	547
Telephones issued	262
Charging sets issued	162
Switchboards issued	23
Wavemeters issued	11

"This is a marvel of the universe;
To fling a thought across a stretch of sky —
Some weighty measure, or a yearning cry,
It matters not; the elements rehearse
Man's urgent utterance..."
J.P. PEABODY

**Evacuation of
Prisoners of War**

"Happy, alas! too
happy."

VERGIL: *Æneid*

ONE MONTH OF REINFORCEMENT & PRISONERS

REINFORCEMENTS RECEIVED
DURING PERIOD 8th FEBRUARY – 8th MARCH

Unit	Officers	O.R.
71 Brigade H.Q.	—	3
4 R.W.F.	9	356
1 Oxf & Bucks	8	195
1 H.L.I.	2	237
158 Bde. H.Q.	—	—
7 R.W.F.	13	346
1 E. Lancs R.	7	141
1/5 Welch R.	9	128
160 Bde. H.Q.	—	1
6 R.W.F.	5	271
4 Welch R.	12	269
2 Mon R.	9	234
53 Reece.	—	7
R.A.	3	7
R.E.	—	18
Sigs.	—	19
1 Manch R.	—	39
R.A.Ch.D.	3	—
Pro.	—	2
R.A.S.C.	1	6
Med.	—	14
Ord.	—	3
R.E.M.E.: H.Q.	—	1
71 Workshops	—	2
158 Workshops	—	3
160 Workshops	—	1
Totals	78	2,103

NUMBER OF PRISONERS OF WAR EVACUATED DURING PERIOD 8th FEBRUARY – 8th MARCH

Date		No.	Through Med. Units
Feb.	9	308	21
	10	327	3
	11	—	12
	12	98	9
	13	96	9
	14	224	3
	16	138	1
	17	—	27
	18	232	9
	19	—	16
	20	190	—
	21	24	—
	24	196	22
	25	220	22
	26	104	6
	27	26	2
	28	22	3
Mar.	1	228	14
	2	—	4
	3	17	3
	4	—	2
	5	119	14
	6	174	—
	7	173	—
Totals		2916	204
		3120	
		+ 50 direct to Corps Cage	
Grand Total		3170	

"God of Battles, was ever a battle like this in the world before?"
TENNYSON: *The Revenge*

THE FIELD CASH OFFICE

"It is not a custom with me to keep money to look at."
GEORGE WASHINGTON

A Divisional Field Cash Office has a staff of one Officer and one N.C.O., and its normal functions during active service are to issue cash to Imprest Holders and individual Officers, and to exchange the currency of the entire Division when it enters a new country. It also receives cash from the Army Post Office, N.A.A.F.I., Y.M.C.A., Canteens, Officers' Shops and from Units for transmission to Banks in the United Kingdom.

Some indication of the number and amount of such transactions is illustrated by the following figures, which are the average for any normal month during action in the recent campaign:

RECEIPTS

	Marks	Sterling equiv.	"Customers"
Army Post Office	1,555,000	£38,875	12
Unit P.R.I. a/c	622,635	£15,565	118
Sundry	344,725	£8,618	20
	2,522,360	£63,058	150

PAYMENTS

	Marks	Sterling equiv.	"Customers"
Unit Imprest a/cs (Soldiers' Pay, etc.)	8,547,800	£213,695	750
Officers' Pay	596,570	£14,914	1,200
Exchanges	82,940	£2,060	270
	9,226,770	£230,609	2,220

A normal Division has approximately 150 Imprest Holders and some 800 Officers. You will see, then, that the daily traffic handled by a Field Cash Office, often housed only in a small tent, consists of roughly 30 Imprest Holders drawing £300 each and 50 Officers drawing £12 each; in the example quoted above, exchanges were only at the rate of 10 per day, all of some £10 worth of currency, but these figures become astronomical when a general exchange takes place on entering a new country.

... and as for the

ARMY CATERING CORPS

"We may live without poetry, music, and art;
We may live without conscience and live without heart,
We may live without friends, we may live without books,
But civilised men cannot live without cooks."

OWEN MEREDITH: Lucile.

— need we say more?

HONOURS AND AWARDS

During the campaign the following immediate awards for gallantry in the face of the enemy were awarded to Officers, Warrant Officers, Non-Commissioned Officers and Men of the 53rd Welsh Division.

V.C.	Major Tasker Watkins, 1/5 Welch Regiment.
D.S.Os.	28.
M.Cs.	124.
D.C.Ms.	24.
M.Ms.	175.

THE RED DRAGON

Altogether 387 issues of the Divisional Newspaper – "Red Dragon" – were published, 334 of these issues being between D Day and VE Day. The average distribution was 1,300 per day, so during the campaign 434,200 copies were distributed in the field. Only on one day was the Division without its "Red Dragon" – at Hornoy just before the crossing of the River Somme – and even then the paper was prepared but rapid movement prevented its publication.

RED DRAGONS CONCERT PARTY

Some time before the invasion of Europe began, it was realised that "live" entertainment for troops in the field was a vital part of the Division's Welfare Services. The original Concert Party of the 53rd Welsh Division "The Roysterers" was joined in 1943, by the "Four by Twos", the Concert Party of the disbanded 42nd Armoured Division. In June, 1943, our Divisional Concert Party under their new name "The Red Dragons" broadcast on the B.B.C. from Woking: in January, 1944, they gave a "Command Performance" at the Queensbury All-Services Club in London. Altogether they gave over 300 shows to the Division prior to D Day.

"What revels are in hand? Is there no play
To ease the anguish of a torturing hour?"
Shakespeare: *Midsummer Night's Dream.*

On D Day itself, members of the Concert Party returned to their own Units (we had, of course no authorised establishment for them, and they were all borne on the strength of Units in the Division) with whom they landed in Europe. On the 30th June they re-formed in Normandy as a Concert Party and immediately began rehearsing their first show, which they gave twice a day for a week at Rucqueville. On this occasion the "theatre", known to everyone as "Wigan Pier", was a barn with a gate for a stage and two three-ton lorries provided the side and back curtains. On many future occasions were they to give shows under such conditions.

From here the Party moved to Le Mesnil Patry, just behind the Divisional Gun Area; here, to the incessant tune of the music of 25-pdrs. and 5.5-inch guns they gave three shows a day for eleven days. Their "theatre" on this occasion was a Dutch barn and they were on

Y DDRAIG GOCH   A DDYRY GYCHWYN

ISSUE NO. 169   MONDAY, 27TH NOVEMBER, 1944

RED DRAGON

D + 174

NO GREAT CHANGE ON WESTERN FRONT

Very little change has taken place on the Western Front during the past 24 hours. Enemy resistance is increasing in some sectors but the Germans have had to give ground in many areas.

In the Venlo area British troops are up to the main defence ring of the town. Three villages have been taken north of Venlo and the enemy has been cleared from all the west bank of the river except a few small pockets. About 40 German parachutists were reported to be fighting a rearguard action in a small strip north of Venlo in a castle. The River Maas is already high and is reported to be rising steadily.

The American 9th Army under General Simpson is fighting hard to hold the two bridgeheads which they have thrown across the River Roer.

In the Geilenkirchen sector (see map overleaf) there has been stiff opposition by enemy artillery and mortar. Yesterday the Americans ,in shelling transport going across the bridge over the River Roer at Linnich scored a direct hit on the explosives with which the enemy meant at some later stage to destroy the bridge. Between Julich and Eschweiler the village of Weisschweiler has been captured after house-to-house fighting. The Germans have brought up artillery and infantry reinforcements in this area. In the Hurtgen Forest American troops have advanced another half mile towards Duren.

One of the Metz forts which has been holding out has now been abandoned by the enemy. General Patton's troops who crossed the River Saar are now seven miles beyond it and are reported to be swinging north. Further south other units of the 3rd American Army are now one mile from St.Avold.

The Americans 7th Army is still pouring reinforcements in men and material through the gap at the northern end of the Vosges mountains. Other 7th Army troops are making good progress all along the Vosges.

General Eisenhower yesterday visited the French 1st Army and toured the front.

- - - - - - - - - - - - - - - -

GERMANS DRIVEN BACK IN BALKANS

The 4th Ukrainian Army which forced its way through the passes into Czechoslovakia and cleared Ruthenia have now captured two more villages in their drive west from Ruthenia. These villages were in a valley and were of great importance to the enemy in this sector.

In northeastern Hungary the advance towards the communications centre of Miskolc continues. Further progress has also been made in the foothills of the Matra mountains. The important road and rail centre of Hatfan between Budapest and Miskolc was captured yesterday after severe fighting.

German reports state that stiff fighting is taking place on the island in the Danube ten miles south of Budapest. The reports also state that the Germans have had to give ground in front of the strong Soviet attacks which are taking place 100 miles south of Budapest. The retreating Germans are being hotly pursued.

- - - - - - - - - - - - - - -

FAR EAST

The 14th Army in Burma has launched a new offensive north of Kalewa. This attack has carried them 12 miles over the upper reaches of the Chindwin river and forward patrols are reported to be another mile beyond. This advance has been made along the road used by the Japanese to carry their supplies during their advance to the Indian frontier.

In northwest Burma part of Bhamo is now in the hands of the Chinese.

Leyte island in the Philippines is being steadily cleared of the Japanese. On Saturday a fourth convoy of reinforcements to Leyte was smashed. This brings the total sent to the bottom by the Allies to 16 four thousand ton transports with all their cargo, 17,000 troops and 14 escorting warships - all bringing reinforcements for Leyte. Yesterday latest reports state that another convoy bound for Leyte has also been destroyed.

- - - - - - - - - - - - - -

LATE NEWS -Tokio has again been attacked by super-fortresses from Saipan. No further details have yet been given.

- - - - - - - - - - - - - -

several occasions machine-gunned by low-flying enemy aircraft, which added excitement to both players and audience – the average audience on these occasions was 300. Without a break they moved to their first real theatre with a stage and curtains at Carpiquet on the outskirts of Caen. Here three live shows a day were given, in addition to two cinema shows a day.

With the break-out from the bridge-head the "Red Dragons" packed up, following closely behind the troops to give shows whenever the opportunity provided itself. Not until they finally reached Antwerp in September, did they settle down for a few days. Here they were not slow to open up in style, and from the stage of the magnificent Empire Theatre with their ranks swelled by Belgian volunteer artistes, they gave ten full-scale shows worthy of London's West End, despite the short time allowed for preparation and presentation.

Nijmegen was the next home of the "Red Dragons" where two shows a day were given for three weeks: further successes followed at Oss, Bree, and Weert, where in November, 1944, they gave one of several Command Performances for Viscount Montgomery of Alamein. From here they moved to winter quarters in the Ardennes where several shows were given in the worst conditions imaginable – many in fact had to be cancelled because the audience were unable to reach the snow bound theatre!

And so back to Holland, the Reichswald battles, the Rhine crossing and the long journey to Hamburg – giving shows here and there wherever possible and battle conditions allowed: they were always there to cheer and amuse battle-weary troops. The last show given by the "Red Dragons" was in Hamburg on the occasion of the farewell visit of General Sir Miles Dempsey to the Division.

During their travels in North-West Europe the "Red Dragons" gave well over three hundred shows (the exact number is not recorded) under all conditions and in all types of fields, barns, halls and theatres. This is indeed a record of which the gallant band of twenty soldiers who composed the Divisional Concert Party can justifiably feel proud.

PAYING THE COST

"Alas! How deeply painful is all payment!"
BYRON: *Don Juan.*

This section tells of the price paid by the 53rd Welsh Division towards its share of the European Victory. In the following pages you will find graphs to indicate comparative casualties of battalions within brigades, of total brigade casualties within the Division, and a summary of all casualties which passed through our Divisional Medical Installations. Altogether 15,074 casualties passed through our Field Ambulances and Field Dressing Stations, of which 7,313 were normal sickness cases, 6,212 were battle casualties, and 1,545 were battle exhaustion cases. To deal with the latter, 13 and 26 Field Dressing Stations were set aside as Divisional Exhaustion Centres. It is interesting to quote here some particulars about the cases handled by these Exhaustion Centres during Operation "Veritable", which lasted for one month (8th February, 1945 to 8th March, 1945). During this period, 485 soldiers were admitted to these centres; of this number, 161 were evacuated to the Corps Exhaustion Centre, 186 were returned to duty with their units, 12 were passed to hospitals, etc., and 14 were retained.

The average percentage of exhaustion cases returned to their units during this operation was 52.4 per cent.

To analyse the casualties sustained by a division in a single campaign is to produce a detailed volume of considerable interest to members of the medical profession. Such is not, of course, our intention here, but we feel that the layman might like to have some idea of the types of cases which pass through division medical installations during a single operation. So once more we will take "Veritable" – the month in and beyond the Reichswald Forest.

During this operation we had a total of 3,484 casualties of all types. These were due to the following causes:

H.E. shell wounds 1,047
Miscellaneous sick 952
Exhaustion cases 485
Gun-shot wounds 359
Mortar bomb wounds 162
Accidental injuries – battle 93
Blast wounds 87
Accidental injuries general 74
General wounds 73
Mine wounds 67
Bomb wounds 39
Battle burns 33
Accidental petrol burns 13

Or perhaps you are interested to know what parts of the body are most vulnerable. In this case we divide the figure of 3,484 as follows:

Lower extremity (including buttocks) 1,038
Upper extremity 700
Exhaustion eases 485
Multiple injuries 305
Miscellaneous 260
Head wounds 216
Abdominal wounds 195

"To preserve a man alive in the midst of so many changes and
hostilities, is as great a miracle as to create him."
JEREMY TAYLOR: *Holy Dying.*

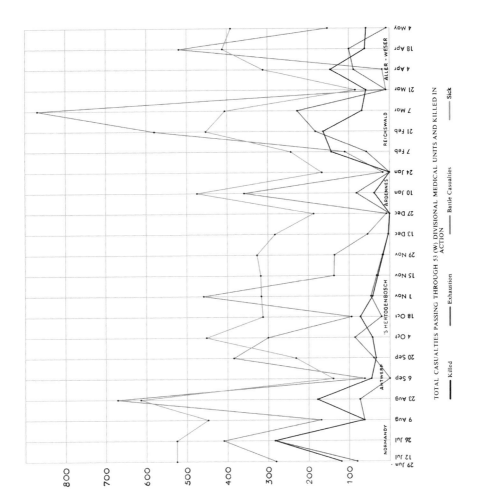

TOTAL CASUALTIES PASSING THROUGH 53 (W) DIVISIONAL MEDICAL UNITS AND KILLED IN ACTION

——— Killed   ——— Exhaustion   ——— Battle Casualties   ——— Sick

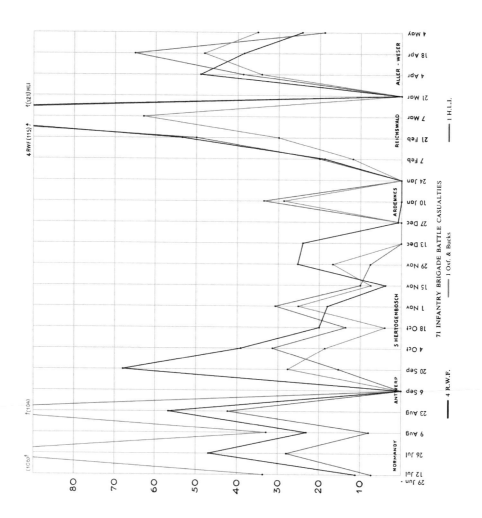

71 INFANTRY BRIGADE BATTLE CASUALTIES

——— 1 H.L.I.   ——— 1 Oxf. & Bucks   ——— 4 R.W.F.

Approach to the R.A.P.

"What wound did ever heal but by degrees."

SHAKESPEARE: *Othello*

SUMMARY OF CASUALTIES DURING OPERATION "OVERLORD"

PERIOD	KILLED		WOUNDED		MISSING		MISSING REJOINED	
	Officers	O.R.	Officers	O.R.	Officers	O.R.	Officers	O.R.
29 June to 12 July	12	89	24	496	4	28	—	18
13 July to 26 July	20	180	51	830	13	332	—	124
27 July to 9 August	6	75	19	350	—	23	1	44
10 August to 23 August	12	178	43	821	3	86	1	50
24 August to 6 September	2	37	9	83	1	21	—	—
7 September to 20 September	6	18	22	480	3	116	—	24
21 September to 4 October	4	30	8	248	—	62	—	25
5 October to 18 October	5	65	14	510	—	14	—	5
19 October to 1 November	3	45	20	250	2	73	—	5
2 November to 15 November	3	33	3	178	2	14	—	10
16 November to 29 November	—	16	4	98	—	6	—	4
30 November to 13 December	1	5	3	48	—	3	—	1
14 December to 27 December	4	7	7	70	—	4	—	1
28 December to 10 January	3	35	16	154	—	15	—	78
11 January to 24 January	—	1	—	—	—	—	—	3
25 January to 7 February	5	130	31	661	—	83	—	50
8 February to 21 February	10	146	36	660	—	70	—	24
22 February to 7 March	2	60	10	201	—	34	—	24
8 March to 21 March	1	48	14	180	—	45	—	10
22 March to 4 April	7	132	34	591	5	202	1	27
5 April to 18 April	3	33	9	150	—	11	—	11
19 April to 4 May	4	33	10	162	—	13	—	15
	113	1396	387	7221	33	1255	3	553

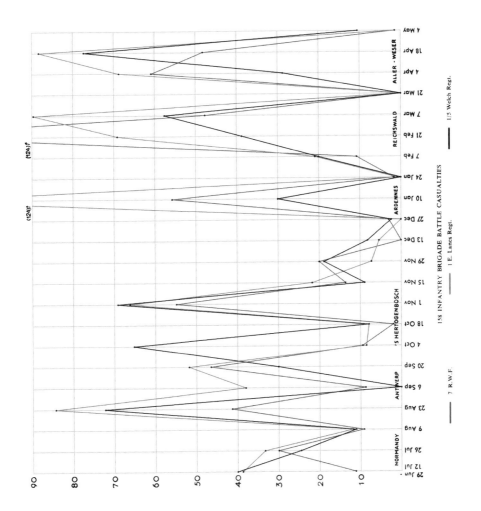

158 INFANTRY BRIGADE BATTLE CASUALTIES

——— 1/5 Welch Regt.

——— 1 E. Lancs Regt.

——— 7 R.W.F.

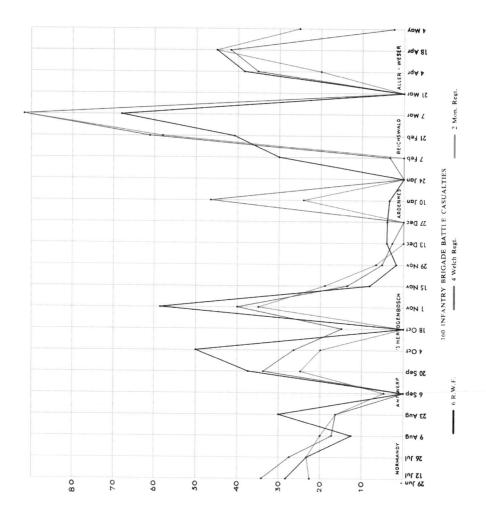

160 INFANTRY BRIGADE BATTLE CASUALTIES

4 Welch Regt.   2 Mon. Regt.

6 R.W.F.

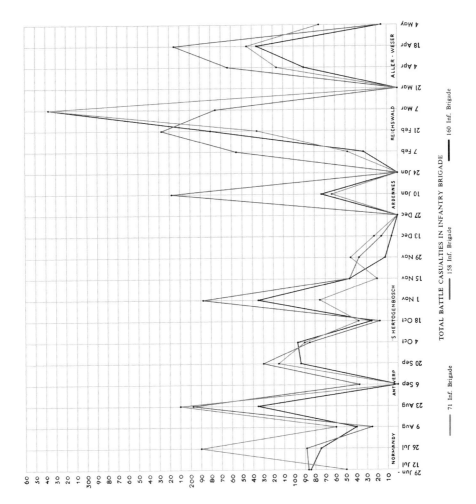

TOTAL BATTLE CASUALTIES IN INFANTRY BRIGADE

——— 160 Inf. Brigade

——— 158 Inf. Brigade

——— 71 Inf. Brigade

"And He gave some Apostles, and some Prophets, and some Evangelists, and some Pastors and Teachers, for the perfecting of the Saints, for the work of the Ministry, for the edifying of the Body of Christ."
New Testament: *Ephesians.*

Before we leave this section, we would like to pay a brief but nonetheless sincere tribute to the work of the Royal Army Chaplains' Department during the campaign.

In an infantry division such as ours there are sixteen chaplains to look after roughly 17,000 men: the result is that they are of necessity thinly spread out in the Divisional area. The team chaplains in this division in 1944 had been brought up to strength for Operation "Overlord" from the 38th Welsh Division. During the course of the campaign there were, in this small team, nine replacements for casualties sustained in the field (one killed and eight evacuated sick or wounded).

The chaplain's work in the field, touching as it does every branch of the soldier's life, cannot well be assessed in bare figures, but those taken from chaplains' records do give some idea of the ground that was covered in preaching the Word and administering the Sacraments:

Number of attendances at services in the field.................. 89,500
Number of Communicants... 14,300
Number of recorded services... 3,780

In addition, two Confirmations were held in the field at Helmond and Eindhoven.

To achieve this, chaplains travelled some 35,000 miles in their cars, in addition to the countless miles travelled on foot.

But so much of the chaplains' work must go unrecorded – their tireless and ever cheerful appearance on the field of battle before, during and after operations achieved a very high morale value: their work in connection with the burial of casualties and attending the wounded under fire will ever remain a shining light in the memory of all who underwent experiences which are too unpleasant to bear recollection.

All these actions on the part of our chaplains did so much to maintain the morale of our troops at a high level that it is difficult to mention them so briefly without digressing, but we would like to mention just one more aspect of their work which was so important to the contentment of mind of the average soldier – his domestic welfare. In addition to their daily work, chaplains handled 1,216 recorded welfare cases and many scores more that were never entered in the record book, only those who have had their domestic troubles solved by the diligent care of the Padre can express their thanks adequately.

Le Bon Repos Crossroads, 1944

" … some corner of a foreign field That is forever England."

RUPERT BROOKE:
The Soldier

LEST WE FORGET

ORIGINAL ORDER OF BATTLE OF 53RD (WELSH) DIVISION DURING OPERATION "OVERLORD"

"I hold it a noble task to rescue from oblivion those
who deserve to be eternally remembered."
Pliny: *Epistles.*

ROYAL ARMOURED CORPS

    53rd Reconnaissance Regiment

ROYAL ARTILLERY

    Headquarters, Royal Artillery

    81st Field Regiment, Royal Artillery

    83rd Field Regiment, Royal Artillery

    133rd Field Regiment, Royal Artillery

    71st Anti-tank Regiment, Royal Artillery

    116th Light Anti-aircraft Regiment, Royal Artillery

NOTE: On 2nd December, 1944, 116th Light Anti-aircraft Regiment was transferred to 50th (Northumbrian) Division prior to disbandment, and 25th Light Anti-aircraft Regiment from that Division joined 53rd (Welsh) Division.

ROYAL ENGINEERS

    Headquarters, Royal Engineers

    244 Field Company, Royal Engineers

    282 Field Company, Royal Engineers

    555 Field Company, Royal Engineers

    285 Field Park Company, Royal Engineers

ROYAL CORPS OF SIGNALS

    53rd Welsh Divisional Signals

INFANTRY

71 *Infantry Brigade*
4th Bn. The Royal Welch Fusiliers
1st Bn. The Oxfordshire and Buckinghamshire Light Infantry
1st Bn. The Highland Light Infantry

158 *(Royal Welch) Infantry Brigade*
7th Bn. The Royal Welch Fusiliers
1st Bn. The East Lancashire Regiment
1st/5th Bn. The Welch Regiment

160 *(South Wales) Infantry Brigade*
6th Bn. The Royal Welch Fusiliers
4th Bn. The Welch Regiment
2nd Bn. The Monmouthshire Regiment
1st Bn. The Manchester Regiment

NOTE: The above Order of Battle came into effect on 3rd August, 1944. Prior to that date 158 Infantry Brigade consisted of all three Battalions of the Royal Welch Fusuilers; the 1st Bn. The East Lancashire Regiment was in 71 Infantry Brigade, and the 1st/5th Bn. The Welch Regiment was in 160 Infantry Brigade.

ROYAL ARMY CHAPLAINS' DEPARTMENT

ROYAL ARMY SERVICE CORPS
501 Company (Infantry Brigade) (25-pdr. ammunition)
531 Company (Infantry Brigade) (Small Arms ammunition)
532 Company (Infantry Brigade) (Supplies)
533 Company (Divisional Troops) (Petrol, Oil and Lubricants)

ROYAL ARMY MEDICAL CORPS
147 Field Ambulance
202 Field Ambulance
212 Field Ambulance
13 Field Dressing Station
26 Field Dressing Station
53 Field Hygiene Section

511 Mobile Dental Unit
529 Mobile Dental Unit
541 Mobile Dental Unit

ROYAL ARMY ORDNANCE CORPS
53rd Welsh Divisional Ordnance Field Park

ROYAL ELECTRICAL AND MECHANICAL ENGINEERS
71 Infantry Brigade Workshops
158 Infantry Brigade Workshops
160 Infantry Brigade Workshops
With eleven Light Aid Detachments and a Light A.A. Workshop

53rd Welsh Divisional Provost Company, Corps of Military Police
53rd Welsh Divisional Postal Unit, Royal Engineers
11th Field Security Section, Intelligence Corps
83rd Field Cash Office, Royal Army Pay Corps

… and we remember too, our friends who served with us in so many of our battles:

79th Armoured Division
4th Armoured Brigade
8th Armoured Brigade
31st Armoured Brigade
33rd Armoured Brigade
34th Armoured Brigade
3rd Army Group Royal Artillery
9th Army Group Royal Artillery
86th Anti-tank Regiment, Royal Artillery
153 Infantry Ordnance Sub-Park
307 Mobile Laundry and Bath Unit
215 Civil Affairs/Military Government Detachment

"These are the soldiers brave enough to tell
The glory-dazzled world that War is hell:
Lovers of peace, they look'd beyond the strife
And rode through hell to save their country's life."
HENRY VAN DYKE

Now are our brows bound with victorious wreaths,
Our bruised arms hung up for monuments;
Our stern alarums chang'd to merry meetings,
Our dreadful marches to delightful measures,
… God, if they will be so,
Enrich the time to come with smooth-fac'd peace,
With smiling plenty, and fair prosperous days!
Abate the edge of traitors, gracious Lord,
That would reduce these bloody days again,
And make poor England weep in streams of blood!
Let them not live to taste this land's increase,
That would with treason wound this fair land's peace!
Now civil wounds are stopp'd, peace lives again;
That she may long live here, God say Amen!

SHAKESPEARE: *Richard III*